You Call this Love?

The Real Reason Women Don't Like Sex

Lisa Bisque

Writers Club Press
San Jose New York Lincoln Shanghai

You Call this Love?
The Real Reason Women Don't Like Sex

Published by Writers Club Press
an imprint of iUniverse.com, Inc.

For information address:
iUniverse.com, Inc.
620 North 48th Street
Suite 201
Lincoln, NE 68504-3467
www.iuniverse.com

ISBN: 0-595-00266-8

Printed in the United States of America

"This book is dedicated to my beloved husband, whom I could not protect."

My sons who inspire, and confirm me everyday of their lives.

My friend, Michele Holt. My first reader, Thank you.

Dr. George Denniston, Thank you for the editorial and moral support.

Patricia Proctor, whose typing skills, and gift of deciphering made this work actually readable. Thank you.

Contents

Prologue

We are the products of our conception. It is where we begin, and we have no say in it. No one has ever had a say. We are vulnerable to the culture and societal customs of the parents we are given to. This is a game of chance with infinite possibilities. Existence in this period of time has dealt us many favorable conditions. We are in the age of true enlightenment, not stigmatized by superstition or ignorance. We have our troubles. Overall though, we have it pretty good. Or do we? We ought to, we seem to know that much. Something is missing, something is not quite right with us, and we all feel it.

This little book will not take up too much of your time. I hope to share reasonable information with reasonable people. In the end, you the reader, will have the ultimate say in what you choose to believe or not to believe.

I have a perfectly clear perception of my existence. Why am I here? Why was I born female to the parents that I was born to? What is my purpose? I have spent many years perplexing over this. My God! What in the world could be the reason for ME being here where I am, and doing what I am doing? I finally gave up fighting something I knew to be true for a long time, and began exploring this reality further. When I opened up to trying to understand my fellow man more honestly, things got much easier for me. This will be apparent to the reader in the second chapter, it is here that I begin telling this story as a male. I have modeled this boy from my husband whom I know better than any other human.

It is my desire that you come away from this book with a better understanding of who we are, what happened to us, and why we are where we are at this time. Hopefully, we will be able to find a better way of dealing with our own feelings, and appreciating the feelings of others

Chapter 1
Common Experience

Man has survived for thousands of years with his foreskin intact. Why, suddenly, is it a bad thing? There is no real proof that a circumcised man is any better off than an intact man. We are now in such a deplorable state, at this point, we must take a new look at an old practice, that has touched every one of us.

Our men are not doing for us sexually and emotionally what we expected. You may outwardly deny this, and scoff, I promise to offer a new view of our sexuality, that you will at least be compelled to consider. We are not happy. This is apparent in all clarity by the way we discuss openly on numerous talk shows, the shortcomings and disappointments we experience in everyday life. Personal and painful disclosures, made public, in hope of some absolution, are attracting listening audiences by the droves.

Nowhere in history has a society been so plagued by our particular troubles. And nowhere in history has a society been able to point to one single manmade disaster that has resulted in the emotional downfall of a civilization. A common experience, that only a few in our generation has escaped.

In America, our males have been singled out systematically and surgically altered in the name of medical progress. As lay people, we have an obligation to re-examine this, as we are so affected on a long-term basis, for the rest of our lives in fact. Lets keep our hearts and minds open to the very real possibility that we have been taken: duped into unnecessary financial loss, physical trauma, emotional trauma, sexual dysfunction and a lifetime of sexual disappointment. This has resulted in male bashing, and female disdain of our male counterparts. I don't believe we really want life to be this way.

Our obligation to re-examine this procedure is vital to our continuation. Our future, and the future of our young depend on our ability to reasonably weigh the enormous risks versus the alleged benefits. The only argument viable for the benefit of circumcision is that 90% of the male babies born have already endured this terrible thing. And, having already endured it, are now faced with living with it the rest of their lives. Knowing the permanence of the situation, we are forced to believe that it has to be good for us. There is no recovering what was once ours that has been taken away. Therefore, we have become comfortable with the lies.

If there could be one issue that would ignite a revolution of thought resulting from the full awareness that the one thing most revered, most prized, had been tampered with irreparably, and that this tampering left us constantly struggling with our sexuality permanently, this would be it.

Our lives and our love relationships have been devastated by one senseless act. The ultimate sexual molestation perpetrated upon us before we were brought home from the hospital.

I speak in terms of we, meaning the suffering continues throughout life, and both men and women are experiencing dire repercussions from this. Long after the initial butchering has forever changed the infant boy, we remain victims of his first real sexual encounter.

I understand the unwillingness of the masses to accept these concepts. It will be very difficult to assimilate. I will not waste your time.

Thank you for your willingness to embark on a journey into understanding and enlightenment. You will never be the same. That is my ultimate purpose, to awaken a nation from a long and fitful sleep.

Chapter

Our Bodies, But Whose Property?

From very early on, we know the protection of our families. Mothers and fathers intent on keeping us safe and unspoiled. A pleasant dream of security, wrapped warmly in the embrace of our parents, they are diligent in their instructions to keep us from harm's way.

"Hold my hand, look both ways before crossing the street, you must wear a helmet and seat belt while riding your bike or traveling in the car. Never talk to strangers or get in a car with someone you don't know. Remember the password."

"Your body is yours, no one should touch you in any way that makes you feel bad."

"Your body is yours. Your body is yours."

At what point in my life did my body become mine, exactly when did I take possession of myself? At birth, before, or sometime after? You see, I know what you had done to me. I am aware that I was deliberately placed in harm's way when I was barely days old. I know this because I bear the scar of this. The proof is clearly visible and there is no plausible deniability. The act was done to me. I did not consent to this. Had I been given an option based on experience and information, I would have been able to decide for myself whether to allow this to happen to me or not.

Alas, no choice was offered. I was born, and I longed to rest from my journey, safe and comforted in your arms. What I faced was an unspeakable horror. A pain forced upon my unsuspecting body so monstrously wretched, I was struck frozen in fear. I was going to die. I could not bear this. Termination was surely imminent.

Although my body did survive, I cried until I was breathless. I was in pain, but I needed to breathe. I must have passed out for I fell into darkness, still tormented by the ache between my legs. I hurt when I moved and I was lost. Alone, yet constantly pursued by the monster that wanted to tie me down and hurt me again.

Terror pursued me, at my back all the time. I know that I could be caught and hurt again. It had happened before, and it could easily happen again because I was small and weak and the beast was huge, stronger than I could ever be, and relentless in its desire to hurt me. I am nothing now. I have no will to resist and resistance is futile anyhow. I will be bested, overcome by a force infinitely more powerful than I. My only option is to succumb.

I continued to survive, but for what I do not know. I can hardly sleep or eat. I hurt all the time. I know there is something seriously wrong with me. When I pass water it burns, when I move my legs my pants rub on me and I am again aware of this, this thing. Someone comes to me when I cry, they pick me up and press me close to them, and though I want this, I am hurting. Its' not so bad now as before, but I swear I can feel everything that touches me there, I can't think about anything else.

You are my mother. I know this now. You help me, and feed me. I am warm and clean. I think I should trust you and I do. You are kind to me, and with you, I am not so very afraid. But I am alone a lot. When I am alone, the beast is back, after me again. I cry, and sometimes you come to me, and sometimes, you don't. I can't depend on you all of the time and I wonder how you really feel about me.

You tell me 'don't cry, big boys don't cry and I need to be a little man'. 'There is no monster in my room, no one, nothing is after me. It is all in my imagination'. Well, I don't want my imagination, I don't want to be alone, with my imagination. I'm so scared.

I can feel myself down there all the time. When I have clothes on, it bothers me; when I am naked, I can feel the air touching me. I have to hold it tight sometimes to make it stop bothering me. I get hit a lot for that. So now I hide when I have to hold me. I can't let anyone see me, 'cause people get real mad at me.

I have to do other things too. I have to go to school. I have to do some chores, and I have to play. I love to play. I think I'll be all right as long as I don't let anyone know I touch myself so much, and I don't let any one know that I am afraid.

It's not easy acting fearless. I do things that make my Mom wild with worry. I jumped off the roof of the house just to prove I could, but I knew it was stupid. It didn't kill me, although it could have and I wouldn't have cared.

Besides, it's my body right? I can be as reckless or careful, as I want to be. Nothing in real life could be as bad as my dreams. In my dreams, I find myself lying flat on my back unable to move. Struggling with all the power I can muster to free myself, and unable to move a muscle. It's like lying in cement as it begins to harden around me. I cannot free myself and no one is there to help. I am alone.

This is fear, and I am not allowed to show fear. At all costs, I will avoid anything or anyone who even hints at shaking me outwardly. My daredevil stunts are of my own design; I can keep danger away by chasing it down. My Mom looks at me sometimes like she doesn't even know who I am. I know she's thinking 'that boy is not right'. I love her and wish she would just hold me close and let me cry some more, but that will never happen. I can't let my dad call me a sissy ever again.

My dad died. Finally I could cry in front of my Mom and brothers and sisters. It was so easy and felt so good. I could cry myself to sleep and it didn't matter if anyone heard me. I really missed my dad, but in a way I was grateful that I could cry. People would understand, at least for a while.

Well, I'm the man of the house now. Ha! Funny, I don't feel like a man. I wonder if I'll ever completely grasp that concept. When I examine my penis, there is this line of discoloration, like the old cut on my shin, darker than the rest of my skin. Right on the head, that runs from one side of the opening more than half way around. And a scar on the shaft that extends from the base of the head back, nearly halfway up the shaft. I think about sex all of the time. And I need to be alone a lot, in case I have to 'uhm' you know.

I like girls, but they don't seem to care much for me. I can't talk to them. I feel like somehow they know about me and they think I'm weird. I know I'm weird. I don't really want to talk much with girls or spend time with them. I really would just like to have sex, and get back to fishing with my friends. They hate me for this.

So I try not to act too interested in them. I wish that getting some wasn't so tricky. Honesty is out of the question, and I don't care much for dishonesty, but it works.

I guess I was about fifteen when I realized I didn't really possess my entire body, it was by accident, and I probably would have been better off not knowing, maybe.

I met someone who was a lot older than me. I liked him and respected him. I felt relaxed in his presence and we talked openly. We had been drinking beer. I laughed so hard at his stories, and for the first time I felt like I belonged to a kind of brotherhood. As guys will do standing around a fire and drinking beer, a 'piss for distance' competition was proposed.

For the first time, I took notice of someone else's parts. I could not believe my eyes. He was huge. I had to know how this was possible. Then he told me. 'Son, you were cut when you were a baby.' "What the fuck are you talking about?" I asked. He repeated to me, 'you were cut'. "When you were probably a couple of days old the doctors and nurses strapped you down, and cut this part of your pecker off." Pulling the skin over the end of his dick, he showed me his foreskin. He might as well have just punched me in the gut. I had the wind knocked out of me, and I felt sick. I didn't know what this was about, but I was fully aware of the scar.

I showed him, and he told me that whoever did it must have been not only mean, but blind as well, cause he'd never seen such a botched up job.

I had waited my whole life for someone to tell me this. I never knew and I always knew. I was never going to have a big one like his. I was cut short and that was the finality of it. No fixing it, no changing it back. My foreskin and blood was trashed in the hospital where I was born. And my parents had paid them to do it.

So I ask you, when do we take possession of our bodies? When does our flesh become our own? Does it even matter-when the body part I care most about was stolen from me, ripped from me, when I was so small and completely vulnerable?

The travesty is, I became responsible for a body I had no control over, ever. I am exactly who I am because of what I endured. I know what you did, you hurt me, robbed me, and told me to get over it, it was nothing. Circumcision of my penis was a decision you made for me because I was your boy and that's what you wanted for me. It was decided and done and I was in a way considered a non-being, incapable of feeling pain or remembering pain. A central player, the victim of your foul bloody crime, and afterward barely given a second thought.

My life has been hell. I have been used. I am not what I should be. My sex life is a disaster. I am painfully aware that I do not satisfy my wife sexually, I am painfully aware that *I* can never fully enjoy sex as nature intended. My wife understands this, and we can talk about it.

* * * * * * * * * *

Millions of men are not so fortunate. Their wives are frustrated and unfulfilled. The divorce rate is proof positive that a man is barely holding on to an existence he is powerless to control or help. Relationships and family adhesion are now just an unattainable fantasy. Failure after failure is gradually eating away at man's inner will. The will is the driving force of existence. Attack the body and the spirit will crumble. This is undeniably evident in the world around us. Just take a close objective look, if you possibly can.

* * * * * * * * * *

A note to our parents: Our lives have been ruined. We are fully aware of the impact that circumcision has had on our lives. The intervention and interference in our bedroom is not appreciated at all. Your act, for whatever reason you care to give, was more destructive than any single other thing that has ever happened to us. You have succeeded only to undermine the quality of our lives, and the lives of our children. Our unhappiness is the core of our existence. Jerry and I can only imagine how things would have been different for us if he was not haunted daily by this extreme loss. Mark me, it is a loss. Something, a part of him he knows he was born with, and knows he was intended to have, was taken from him. The blow is devastating because we both know this could have been prevented. You had no right to do this, and the lives we live, the thoughts we think and our future has been marked and marred by the past. Thanks for nothing.

Chapter

Violence, Children Learn What They Live

Society is faced with an epidemic about which the CDC in its present collective state of mind is unwilling to do anything about. We are not dealing with a virus or pathogenic microbe. These at least can be identified and some defenses instituted to curb its invasion.

The current threat is so subtle, and yet couldn't be a more "in your face" problem. Violent children, gender/race specifically speaking, white male children. A rash of crime sweeping the nation, so brutal, so heinous as to leave us emotionally shocked and stupefied on a national scale.

We watch horrified as newscasters bring us word of mass killings. The victims are children, confidently entrusted to the sanctuary of school, a place where our worst fear is a playground injury or fight. The reality is mass murder and terrorism acts. Dead and dying at the feet of teachers who are helpless to protect them from the attacks of their own classmates.

The attackers, are mere children themselves. Adolescent boys armed surprisingly well, calculating, deliberate, jubilant, and apparently happy with the sensation of supreme power, instilling fear, and the bone chilling terror of impending death.

What provokes the desire to commit mass murder and mayhem? Is the answer so complex as to be unanswerable? Are we at the mercy of these random explosions, erupting so unpredictably? A scattering of terrorism brought about by bright promising young men. Shocking because of the brutality. The symptoms of an underlying personal catastrophe are generally well masked by a generally benign exterior.

Things seem to be in order, usually no serious troubles in the history of the child. Perhaps isolated incidents of harassing or teasing. A rejection by a perceived girlfriend, a self-imposed exile to the bedroom in front of the computer. Communication on a non-personal level, cyber-relationships in which he feels accepted and respected. His personal relationships are inconsummate and sterile. Rejection in this forum, on this level is eliminated.

Life should be good though. Usually there is enough money and security that would preclude the issue of poverty and deprivation as probable cause. We learn that popularity and attraction of the opposite sex is lacking. Girls are a total mystery to them, and their personal interactions are suffering.

Rejection, and fear of rejection, drive them deeper within themselves and further away from connection to others on an intimate plane.

A severe self-esteem deficiency, low self-confidence and feeling of inadequacy permeate their being. From where this came no one is willing to say, or able to say. Society tells them they should be confident and tough and must overcome obstacles to succeed. Feelings of inferiority must be resisted, repressed and not discussed.

At the forefront of success is the sexual issue. A man is only as good as his ability to relate to and attract females. If he is successful here, he will excel in other areas of interest. In fact, if he is successful in relationships and his interactions with girls and women are satisfying, he is accepted by his male contemporaries, and is free to pursue fulfillment in his intellectual field of interest.

If he is unsuccessful, his entire being is in conflict to reconcile the problem. He is at a total loss to identify the cause of the problem and therefore wrestles with an impenetrable blockade of uncertainty and confusion. What's wrong with me? Why can't I have the thing I need most?

Of course, boys won't discuss this inner conflict, and so no means of resolution is at our disposal. Questions go unasked, and answers go unspoken. In rare instances the subject may be broached, but usually it is discounted as an insecurity, that as a male he is to overcome in his own masculine way. A show of insecurity or a verbalization is shunned, he is turned away to work it out on his own, be a man about it. Words and rebuttals he probably has heard before, and so may never share his feelings with anyone. I am convinced the root of these very male, very intimate dilemmas is without a doubt, the result of unbridled brutality inflicted in the first days of life. The very next sensation following the trauma of birth itself, is the excruciating attack upon his delicate and innocent penis. The very crux of his future manhood is unabashedly attacked with a fierceness his tiny body and immature mind cannot comprehend. He suffers, he screams, he is tied down and helpless to escape. How can this be forgotten? The human psyche is so complex that science is at a loss to explain decisively what makes us who we are. Most people agree we are spiritual beings. What greater hurt to the spirit can be inflicted than this act of sadistic mutilation? Our boys fight back as infants the only way they can. They cry. Still the pain continues even after their exhaustion consumes their tiny violated selves.

Doctors and professionals insist that the pain is transient and the scarring is insignificant psychologically and physically. Who are they to say? Can we admit the medical profession has been wrong about so many other things, and then adamantly insist they are right on this? The evidence is in the way we are losing our boys to a host of inner demons they are powerless to identify, and even less able to talk about.

The killing will continue I promise you that. We will continue to bear witness to the sorrowful loss of innocent lives claimed by a rage so intense and so destructive, our only hope of comfort will be in our own demise.

Violence is repaid with violence. Our sons are in a position to inflict pain and suffering on a mass scale unparalleled in history. Automatic weapons, explosives, and information are at their disposal.

Most boys do not come to this end, many suffer in silence, forcing themselves to behave acceptably, masking their pain and fear, sometimes living their entire lives in torment, and sometimes resorting to suicide as the ultimate release from their pain.

Though all do not resort to violence, I am certain that all feel this pain. However remote or repressed there is still an inner part of their spirit that remembers "something horrible happened to me and I was devastated." Time, growth, nurturing and conditioning have put these feelings deep inside, almost gone, but never truly forgotten. For the spirit is forever in touch with all things that affect us, both good and bad.

Drugs and alcohol help to numb.

This pain of circumcision is an evil thing that will remain deep in the memory, subconsciously as an evil that must be addressed somehow. The sad manifestations are the acts of violence and very real harm that our children perpetrate upon others, people known to them, and strangers.

After all there were no identifiable attackers this baby could hold accountable. In his mind it was a random act inflicted by a group of strangers. Bad people for sure. No one he knew or cared about and certainly no one that cared about him.

So when the blast of the AK-47 or the bomb or the cannon hits anyone and no one in particular, the roulette wheel of pain has simply stopped on someone else, and this time he is the one who spins the wheel! Triumph, revenge, and the taste of blood are now in his mouth. He did not ask for this, he did not want it, but he is a pawn in a game he was born to lose.

Random, senseless acts of violence and brutality; children definitely learn what they live! I have no proof that the children who have committed these acts were themselves victims of routine circumcision. My heart tells me that they were. You see the practice is on the decline, but the numbers, the percentages, are still very high. The chances a baby will not come under the scalpel are not in his favor. Escape is only a matter of luck and when the numbers are about 60-40 against him, I am inclined to speculate that the pain and rage are from somewhere deep inside, a result of an ambush he himself endured.

This information may not have even been asked, the possibility not publicly broached. I would like to know.

If I am wrong, I'll cede that these particular boys had other issues tormenting them. Perhaps they were not victimized themselves and they were just conceived and born evil in a society that glorifies violence, and the combination resulted in melee.

If they were intact, we must not be swayed in our conviction that routine infant circumcision has any merit.

It is still cruel and unusual and must be stopped. But if they were *not* intact...

C h a p t e r

Control, Money and the Baby Boom

"The Baby Boom and Medical Atrocities:

When World War II was finally over and the US fighting machine came home to their women, a mighty wave of humanity sprang forth from the reunion. The entire nation conceived at the same time. Tens of thousands of couples were doing it regularly and successfully.

The medical community was now in a prime position to sell their product to the masses on a scale that would make them millionaires in just a matter of months.

Community hospitals were erected and expanded in every city in America. Maternity wards became the place to give birth, and childbirth was miraculously changed from a naturally occurring bodily process into a dangerous life threatening illness that now required women to seek and obtain professional life-saving interventions.

The concept was cleverly marketed and sold, approved and recommended by the government. The process of pregnancy and birth was best left up to the professionals now.

Public opinion was effectively swayed and women flocked to the hospital to have their babies. The horrors that awaited them were state of the art and top of the line.

Drugs. Lots of drugs. Drugs to induce labor, drugs to stop labor, drugs to completely deaden the pain of labor and delivery. Drugs to dry the milk in the breast. Everyone who could possibly turn a buck by completely changing this natural function into a managed financial cash cow was jumping in on it.

For instance, women were encouraged to bottle feed babies. The benefit to the mother was that she could maintain modesty while feeding the baby in public and her breasts would remain at the pre-pregnant height and firmness. Wow! Freedom and vanity for the mother!

Who else benefited? Well, for starters, the companies that were canning milk products, the bottle and nipple manufacturers, pharmaceuticals that made millions in providing the drugs to stop natural milk production, and baby food manufacturers.

The trade-off for women was colicky babies, fat and malnourished babies, endless hours sterilizing bottles and mixing formulas. Fractured bonding between mother and child, and disconnection of spirit.

The labor and delivery nightmare. Separation from familiar support systems, shaving of the pubis completely.

Drugs. Surgery. Episiotomies—a cutting of the vagina to enlarge the birth canal to speed the baby's passage and if that weren't quick enough, they would reach in with metal forceps and grab the baby by his head and pull him out. After-care of mom included a few stitches to close the episiotomy, and for the benefit of Dad, a few extra to insure a tight fit.

This has all been brought up before. I am only mentioning it as a reminder.

It was in this environment that routine circumcision evolved. It was decided that this could be another means of getting a few extra bucks out of every mother of a newborn boy. The procedure had been done in other cultures with little risk to the baby. Now, how to sell this product to the public? So the campaign began. It's cleaner, it inhibits male masturbation, and it prolongs the sex act. Every one is doing it and you wouldn't want your son to be embarrassed because he looks different. It has no effect on the baby, babies can't feel pain, and it is safe. It prevents cancer.

Moms were on drugs and fathers weren't permitted to attend births. Restrictions were imposed to further separate the family, denying input into these decisions. Those were the hospital rules. I think the drugs, and gender inequality, had a big influence. Women were under the influence, and doctors had absolute control of the entire game. When the respected and revered doctor made a claim such as this, the mom was so swayed as to agree. She did not have a medical degree and so had no authority or experience to make a sound judgment. She did what she was told and accepted the advice of her doctor. Doctors believed they were doing the right thing too. I hope.

The cruelty of circumcision is indisputable. Only a heartless bastard could condone and encourage this. Animals are treated with more respect and kindness than our baby boys.

Mistakes were made, baby boys were killed and their deaths covered up. Baby boys were hurt so badly that they had to be surgically changed into little girls. This was rare, but it happened. Less severe mistakes were made too, and it never should have happened in the first place.

Circumcision is a surgery, and it has risks. People really need to question the necessity of placing their newborn in such a vulnerable position. Surgery is by definition medically necessary to save the life or limb of the patient. Circumcision of the newborn infant does not qualify as a life saving measure and therefore is an unethical act, committed by unscrupulous practitioners for profit.

Chapter 5
Hygiene

This is something all readers will appreciate. The prevailing reasoning for the argument in favor of circumcision is hygiene. It is cleaner. Does this mean we owe our parents and the medical practice of the times a debt of gratitude because our men are cleaner?

God knows that men are stupid and dirty, totally incapable of washing themselves regularly. Therefore, for their own good, we have fixed this problem so that they will be cleaner. Thank goodness the age-old question of male hygiene has been duly noted and addressed. Mothers will never have to approach the unsavory embarrassing task of teaching their boys that they must wash their penis.

I am sure that this has been a traumatic part of raising boys from as far back as Eve's time and women have struggled and fretted over this to the point of tears. Overcome by shame and disgust, they have been offered a solution to this.

They hustled their baby boys to the waiting circumcision restraining board for the solution.

All men should also find themselves grateful, as now with your new and improved penis, the tiresome and tedious job of washing yourselves is ancient history. No sir! No more soap and water on this baby.

I hope you appreciate this. I mean really appreciate this. Imagine what life would be like if you had to wash your dick EVERY DAY! You might have found yourselves missing a great deal of life's other joys.

Circumcision, pardon the pun, has literally "shaved" hundreds of hours off of your personal hygiene regimen. And now all that time and effort can be put to better use, such as trying to find someone to be really interested in your squeaky clean tool!

As a woman, I am relieved that the medical profession has not pondered, and persued the surgical alteration of my private parts. Imagine if they decided that the collection of secretions on and around my clitoris was so vile, that the best way to eliminate this problem is to surgically remove my clitoris, along with the surrounding folds of skin. Do this to me as an infant, so that I would never know the sensation of a clitoral orgasm and therefore not even miss it. If a person can think of doing it, what set of standards of prevention could stop it?

Admittedly this seems rather extreme, doesn't it? We all know that a woman's intimate parts are a source of unpleasant odors and sickness, and that thorough cleaning with hundreds of scented feminine hygiene products and medicated douches are necessary. To the extent of taking up several aisles of the supermarket, they are produced and marketed to keep this problem under control. Hours of television commercials are dedicated to making women aware of their problems of hygiene, and what products are out there on the market that will eliminate this problem, on a temporary basis only, because the site becomes foul and must be tended to daily. This daily bombardment of information on the female condition and the methods of dealing with it are a source of embarrassment to me. I am a mother of three sons who watch TV. They see this and they absorb this information. My husband tells me, "Look at this! Women must be the filthiest creatures on the planet, and I was cut so that I could be clean!" Where is the logic in this? I answer him by saying, "Excuse me, I need to go douche, O.K.? I don't have time to talk to you about this, I have to wash."

But doesn't it offend you just a little bit? I mean, don't you feel at least a twitch of uneasiness about this?

If all the reasons mentioned for circumcising had any basis in fact or truth, I would not be suffering this painful writer's cramp. But since every argument for this practice is rooted in false and misleading propaganda, I am compelled to press on.

In closing this chapter on cleanliness, a reminder from your mothers. Sons, be sure to wash yourselves daily and thoroughly and don't feel bad about yourselves if you actually like it.

Chapter

Less Is More—Common Sense About Quantities

This will be the most difficult of concepts to grasp. I am certain that most everyone is going to vehemently deny this possibility. I have heard this before and no doubt will hear it again. One thing has nothing to do with the other. In nearly all my conversations with people, I have been vigorously rebutted.

Well here goes one more try! Circumcision at birth severely reduces the size of the penis at maturity! This is my statement. I know this to be true by my own observations, and as yet have not seen a circumcised penis that impressed me to alter my stance on this one bit.

Now the scientific mathematical truths that bear out this statement. (I know you are thinking she's crazy—circumcision does not in any way affect the size of the penis).

Well if that is absolute truth and you believe it, then go on and live happily in your little garden by the sea. I'm sure the Easter bunny is enjoying your company.

Mathematically speaking, if you are right that one has nothing to do with the other, then this is a modern miracle of world changing proportions. You see, the penis is the only source from which a part can be taken away, cut off from, and what is left is exactly the same amount as what was started with. Amazing feats of modern medicine has now provided us with the unshakable truth that when we remove a portion of a whole, what we are left with is still whole.

Not less than, not smaller than, not affected at all. One has nothing to do with the other! What a discovery! News to share with the world. Are we here in America brilliant or what? Collectively, we deserve the Nobel Peace prize for this bit of information. Think of the implications. We can now begin to subtract money from our checking accounts and keep the balance fixed at whatever amount we desire. Suck oil from the ground without ever worrying about running out. Consumption will be a thing of the past, once we put these principals to work in other critical areas of our lives. The fear of depletion and scarcity will become an outdated trifling.

I, for one, am all for this. I can easily see how this could catch on in my daily life. Any one who wants to argue counter to what I say to be true, is crazy. Oh, and leave the Easter Bunny and Tooth Fairy out of this, they are personal friends of mine.

Well, people, I know you were hoping for me to join you, and while it must be a blessed state of mind, I cannot go with you there. I am in the real world where subtraction is a steadfast fact of life that does not play favorites, and apply itself to certain situations just because we wish it to. The fact is, that when a portion of something is removed from the whole, what you have left is the remainder, and the remainder will always be less than what was started with.

This is not specific to everything else conceivable except the penis. No, the principal holds true for the male genitalia as well. The foreskin is the fold of skin that is continuous with the skin on the shaft of the penis. When the penis is fully erect, the foreskin is no longer visible as it was when the penis is flaccid. As the penis grows to erection, the cavernosum becomes engorged with blood. The foreskin retracts, the head of the penis becomes exposed. There is no "extra skin". The cavernosum will engorge to the extent allowed by its covering.

The more skin available to contain the cavernosum, the larger the erect penis. The foreskin allows more room for blood engorgement, and results in a more comfortable erection. Many circumcised men have been cut so tightly, they experience painful erections.

This is pretty basic stuff, and this is how the penis works. When the foreskin is cut off, blood vessels are interrupted, and the ability for growth is severely limited by the lack of this skin. In an infant it is not much skin, for an adult that same foreskin is 12-15 square inches. The size of a 3x5 index card! There is nothing extra on a real hard man. He simply has more than he would if he'd been cut.

Now I'm not saying that every intact man is a foot long or better. Everyone is different. Some men are longer, some are thicker, but the foreskin is a natural occurrence. The removal of this in infancy is going to decrease the size of the penis considerably, thus forever altering sexual mechanics. And if you were to ask a man would he prefer that his penis were larger than what it is, I'm sure the answer would be an overwhelming "No! I wish that my penis were much smaller than it is now." Again, say hi! to the Easter Bunny for me.

Chapter 7
Religion and Original Sin

Man has sought a spiritual connection with a supreme and loving being. An entity that comforts when there is conflict. Our religion should be a source of comfort and protection. The gospel of love should be central to this binding of community.

What we have is a judgmental threatening aura of imminent punishment and spiritual abandonment. In my experience, I heard love but felt wrath.

Our spiritual leaders are corrupt and wealth seeking and out of touch with our troubles. Out of touch because they condemn without mercy the behaviors and lifestyles of people they know or care nothing about.

Compassion, understanding and an earnest desire to seek out the possible causes of these behaviors should be the cornerstone of modern spiritual leadership. Instead we have a preoccupation of judgment and damnation.

Where were the religious leaders at the time when our babies needed them most? Where was the voice of reason and compassion that should have shouted from the rooftops—"stop this?" This custom is not our custom. These practices are not part of the teachings of our New Testament savior.

Yet what happened? At what point did the gentile people accept this? And why?

Well I suppose accountability is going to be vague at best. Everyone will share some blame in this. After all even today I look around and see heads in the sand and asses in the air.

I am not anti-Semite. I am anti-circumcision. It is the practice of genital cutting I am trying to eliminate.

ORIGINAL SIN.

You may reject this if you like.

I have frequently asked myself what could motivate a man to conceive of such an act of circumcision in the first place. What possible gain could he as a man hope to achieve? What feeling or emotion could benefit a man from this act of self-mutilation?

I had an incredible eye popping revelation upon waking one recent morning. I was stirred by man's belief in original sin. From scripture we know that the serpent initiated original sin and in Eve's temptation, by her seduction, man was outcast from his God. It was she that brought about his greatest suffering, a loss of communion with his creator. A loss so great, so wounding of spirit, he never recovered.

He was cursed by God to toil, to earn his way and bread by the sweat of his brow.

God's punishment on women is pain in childbearing.

There is no doubt in my mind that man was devastated by this loss. He was an outcast shamed by his nakedness and forced to hide. Humiliated when asked by God what was wrong, he replied, "it's her fault. She tasted and offered it to me. I did not resist."

Of course, I wasn't there and I don't know the exact words that were said. I am no doubt taking liberties based on what I have learned in my religious training. Who out there doesn't take liberties with the word of God?

Now man is on his own. He has his woman. She is good for him and tries to comfort him. They struggle with their independence and no doubt, both have some regrets. She suffers pain in childbirth true to God's promise, and she bears this as stoically as possible. Perhaps it is this stoicism that so riles him.

Well, generations pass and man has troubles. His comfort is the gift of lovemaking and both he and she are taken to new heights of ecstasy in the act. She is happy with him and the lovemaking is extremely pleasurable for her. She is enjoying herself immensely by his touch and he is fully aware of her power over him and ability to direct him to this plane of sensation so wonderful, so beautiful, that he can almost forget his loss. In fact, at times he does and when he realizes that the act may drive him further from his God, he begins to question the righteousness of this. He has doubts as to his right to such happiness, and hers too. After all, she is the reason we are in this fix. Could this be another temptation of the serpent? God warned us of his presence in our lives; told us that he would constantly pursue us. If this has the power to cause me to forget my fall from Grace, can this be a tool of the serpent? It is so good, it must be evil.

What then to do about it? What indeed? I spend a good deal of time with her, hours even, my work suffers and I don't mind, but I should. The house is a wreck and that's all right too. What time is left I must rush to do chores, farm, shepherd the flocks and so on and so on.

Can I make peace with my God by somehow sacrificing this pleasure? Is there a way I can break this hold she has on me so I can reconnect with my God? Something surely must be done. If I can somehow diminish her pleasure can I lessen the time I take with her to pursue my quest of absolution? Is this possible?

Perhaps the struggle for the answer was so intense and so sincere that the answer was also revealed in a dream or message. Yes, by cutting off of the foreskin of your penis, you can have what you want. All that you desire is to somehow get back to God and this is the means to that end. She will allow it because you are her man; you have dominion over her, not the other way around. Okay, it is done. I will take charge and order it to be done to all future generations as well. But it must be done in infancy because people in their right mind won't accept this, and it must come as a direct order from God or it will not fly. With proper instruction, the practice will perpetuate and the whole nation will benefit on a spiritual level. Women will not miss what they never had and men will continue to glean pleasure from the act. But not so much he is distracted from his work or spiritual pursuits.

* * * * * * * * * *

Now history is made and I am clearer on the motivation. I am compelled to contemplate such a question because I am forced to live with the consequences. I have no religion to back me up to compensate for my loss; I have no such support system. Yet I must live with the consequences.

I miss natural sex. I had it and I know what it is, and it tears me to pieces that I can't have it. What am I supposed to do? How do I live with my lot in life? Tell me what happened to me and give me a real reason that I can accept. Something that applies to me.

Chapter

Sex Crimes and Self-Control

Once again, I must state we are in a society awash in chaos. We would like to believe that we are more civilized than at any other time in history. We are better educated, better informed and despite this information and education, we are ripped apart by crime.

The sex crimes of this century are appalling. We are all excruciatingly aware of the horrific nature of these sex crimes. The trends are toward a worsening of this problem too. The victims and assailants are getting younger and the cover up attempts are worse than any tales from the crypt.

Men who commit sex crimes are not all victims of circumcision. That would be a sweeping generalization that would be incorrect and irresponsible. However, we can not deny that many sex offenders who are circumcised may very well have been righteous citizens if they had not been placed in front of the train.

I can tell you that it is within the realm of possibility that circumcised sex offenders have acted out of an unquenchable desire to fulfill themselves, and that their acts are a direct result of post traumatic circumcision stress disorder. They have been driven to debauchery by a force strong and unrelenting, and were at a loss to tell us any more than, they were compelled to do what they did to satisfy an urge they were powerless to quell. This is not a pardon for their crimes, but an insight, an offering of an idea, a plausible theory. Case studies and histories aside, you cannot study something that people are completely unwilling to address as an issue in the first place.

I hope that I am right. In fact, I am sure I am right for I know that circumcision is wrong. What do we have to lose by just discontinuing the practice on all members of the human race?

Just stop doing it now, and allow the boys an even chance in life. We can work out the proving of the debate as we go. Don't worry about how your child will feel compared to others; be confidant that he will be capable of washing himself. Let the child have a chance at life without the pain. If he chooses to want it later, take pride in yourselves for allowing him the decision, instead of forcing him to live with your choice over his body. You can never defend yourself if he decides that he would have preferred this to be left up to him, and you took that option from him.

Sex, drugs and alcohol all are very much a part of our lives. Drugs and alcohol are often used to enhance the sex,

or to numb the pain of a sexually dysfunctional life. It may not begin that way, but as life goes on the disappointment with that one thing that would sustain us becomes too great a cross to bear, and escape from our loss is mandatory, for madness is on the verge of permanently overtaking us.

Intelligent, pertinent surveys should be conducted. An unbiased and honest quest to determine if there is a correlation between infant circumcision and a male who has a need to be violent, consumed by rage.

I believe our first mistake is in the act itself. That is followed by the belief that the practice is harmless and there is no need to address it further afterward. The child could be emotionally and psychologically bent forever, but that one thing has nothing to do with the other. The child does not even have a right to the truth, much less any instruction on how to live with it after. His odd behaviors, violent fits, withdrawal, will not even be considered a result of the so-called harmless mutilation of his body.

His perverted preoccupation with his sex is a result of his own mental illness, a natural occurrence not something created in him by his doctor and parents.

I can't believe we have to remain so closed minded about this. Wouldn't it be a relief to anyone to know that your son's problems may and could very well be directly linked to a cause he had no control over? Wouldn't it bring some peace of mind to know that he was not born wicked and that he acted on a compulsion born of his own innocence torn asunder. We have done a terrible disservice to our sons and they deserve better. The least we can do is attempt to search for the truth. Find out for certain that there is a negative consequence that results from a negative action.

Chapter 9
Ancient Custom, Modern Catastrophe

Certainly no one was questioning the quality of his or her son's sex life at the time of his birth. We knew that the procedure would not interfere with his ability to procreate, and therefore this circumcision thing would really have no effect on him as a man. "It makes no difference at all physically," we were told and our parents were told. What did they care? Most were enjoying natural sex and it was good for them. They believed that line about it making no difference, and so the decision for them was easy. They believed they were getting what was best for their children. What their children got left with was a life fraught with unprecedented girl-boy trouble. As sons and daughters of this practice grew into their sexuality, the procedure had now become a mainstay. It was practiced on such a wide scale; it simply, excruciatingly, perpetuated into a plague on future generations.

At one point, boys did not look like their fathers, and one generation was different from the other. Fathers were intact and sons were circumcised. There was a campaign to get to the fathers as well. A rumor was circulated that circumcision would prolong the sex act. By the exposure of the glans, the penis would gradually become desensitized and require more friction to reach orgasm. This assertion is quite questionable since so many American men have problems with "premature ejaculation". But since all of us are looking to improve our sex and will resort to extreme measures to accomplish this, many men consented to be circumcised as adults. This occurred in the late '50's. I can't prove it on a national scale, but the divorce rate began to escalate at an alarming rate not too long after this campaign began. The American family began to disintegrate shortly after the circumcision craze took hold.

The breakdown of the family unit has since become another mainstay of American life. People will meet, fall in love, have a few babies together and then decide this is not working for me. I am not happy with you anymore and I probably never was, so it's time to pack your clothes and get out. I have to move on and try to find what's missing in my life and you certainly don't have what I'm looking for, so beat it. Daddy gets kicked out and mom gets a boyfriend. Then he gets kicked out, and another boyfriend comes along.

Eventually mom gets sick of boyfriends and other husbands and is now alone, or still searching.

The kids are left in a wake of personal relationship disasters. Growing up into their own sexuality, falling in love, getting married, having a couple of kids and then they decide, this is not working for me. I am not happy with you anymore and I probably never was, so pack your bags, and get out. I have to move on and try to find what's missing in my life and you just don't have it. Now beat it. Daddy gets kicked out, and mom gets a boyfriend.

Our base requirement for sexual gratification has driven generations of us to commit acts of sexual depravity and vicarious participation in acts of homosexuality, bestiality, pedophilia and you name it. The pornography industry is not really the cause of sexual debauchery, but only a symptom of a people who are lacking the ability to achieve sexual harmony in the way we were intended. Our sex as adults is perverted because our sex as infants was perverted.

We can fix this by recognizing the cause for what it is and committing ourselves to a better future for our children. We can deal with this catastrophe. Of course what is cut already will remain cut, but by stopping the butchery now, and giving our sons an even start in life, perhaps we will be able to see a change in our lifetime. A natural reversal of trends is possible through the acceptance of this fundamental truth. We owe it to our children to at least try it. At present we are in a downward spiral and no one has been able to suggest any real hope for us. Experts, theologians, politicians and voters all agree we are in a world of trouble. They are capable of identifying the troubles and naming the evils specifically, yet no one has been able to say definitively that **this** is the reason we are in so much trouble. **This** is the one thing that has had a negative impact on everyone and if we stop this now, we can negotiate a turn around. We can redirect the course of our future world. Society can be better. Immorality can be curbed.

These are the words we need to hear, this is the message we long for, isn't it? We need to be told that there is a solution, that a causative factor has been identified and we are making changes as we speak. We need someone to come forward and lead us back to a clearer and more defined path. Acceptance is the key. Stubbornness and closed minds will only insure our continued downward pitch.

People are going to need each other for support. Love and forgiveness will have to be our tools to recovery. For that is what we are headed for. A wave of grieving for our loss will overcome us and we must be ready to help each other. It is a matter of utmost urgency that we accept responsibility for our maltreatment of each other, ask forgiveness and be ready to grant forgiveness.

Then only can healing occur. We must see one another through our new eyes of compassion, recognizing each other as products of someone else's design and not really ourselves. For it is without a doubt that all of us, men and women, would have been different if we had been left unscathed by this scourge of modern civilization.

Chapter 10
Masculinity—Femininity, No Distinctions

Maleness, the basic quality that attracts females, is strength, confidence, bravado, pheromones, unseen attractions, and chemistry; this draws men and women together.

For a long time the quality has been noticeably lacking. Natural attraction is a mere hint of a storybook affair. The magnetism and power, meaning the real power of sensuality that women naturally respond to, is gone from our modern men. We are gradually losing touch with the irresistable mutual desire that we were promised. Our hearts and minds know that courtship and sensual desire are supposed to be like a drug that we need and pursue.

Yet at every turn, women are disappointed by man's inability to capture her heart with a promise of pleasure, yet undeliverable. The reality of this act of lovemaking is repeatedly disappointing, and "faking it" is becoming more and more difficult, knowing ahead of time that the love-making is going to fall far short of wonderful. The pursuit and attainment of romantic love is only subject matter in romance novels—not a reality of life.

I believe that women really want to feel they are safe with and protected by a man. That she wants to rely upon his strength and relax her guard with him, knowing in her heart he is strong and capable and willing to go to the mat for her. What we are getting is a weakling; a person easily bowled over at the slightest hint of confrontation or bodily harm.

It is very difficult to respect a man who is like this. If he cannot be looked to for strength, there goes the respect and finally the desire to have sex.

As males and females, we are born to certain character-istics that cannot be denied. We have certain expectations for each other and what we are being told is that the old stereotypes relating to maleness should be altered to accommodate the new man. Our standards should be low-ered to allow for core weakness and vulnerability. Feminine characteristics should be celebrated and accepted. Yet this is contrary to our natural tendencies. Now women are confused and frustrated. We want to stay in love with the image of the man we are drawn to. We want to respect him and we don't want him to relinquish the role as protector and leader of the clan.

Over time, these basic needs drive us to seek the male we dream of, desire with all our hearts. We wind up throwing away a man who truly does care about us, but is powerless to be the male we need. A sad, tragic place to be, only to search out and find another cut from the same cloth, as few young men were spared.

Femininity, It's Not Just For Women Anymore—For years feminine characteristics have been easily identified in boys. Even when I was a kid I could see that boys were odd. They just didn't seem right to me. Maybe the female characteristics were not that apparent, but the geekiness has always been there.

When I went to school, boys still had a modicum of their societal superiority over girls. They lost ground fast though, and today boys are trifled with to such extremes that the gender has practically blended itself into the female population.

A woman can easily dominate the spirit of a man and manipulate him into doing just about anything for her sex. The role reversal is so much a part of our society; we accept it as the natural course of our destiny. Women are sick of men that cannot support us, and lose themselves in drugs and alcohol. We have thrown them out of our lives. We have become willing to burden the responsibility of raising a family alone rather than put up with a weak sick boy in a man's body.

We see all things wrong with him and blame him solely for his shortcomings, never willing to look at the possibility that he is in a position he can't get out of, and that he is not responsible for the way he is. In fact, we tend to be more steadfast in our conviction that this condition is unique to our generation, and that no one thing, no single occurrence is at the root of our situation. We believe what we have been told. That circumcision is harmless, beneficial and has no lasting consequence.

Still our boys grow into adulthood at war with this sex thing and torn asunder with confusion. Homosexuality is a mainstay—a fact of life. Sex is necessary and if fulfillment is not possible in the natural traditional male—female order of things, then it will be sought after and attained by any means available.

Alternate lifestyles are now a choice being made more often than expected in nature. Boys are choosing to be partners with each other earlier and are not even giving themselves a chance at heterosexual relationships.

Our men are giving up on the natural order because they feel unnatural. They are painfully aware that they may not make the cut as a man's man, and so quit before the chance of humiliation from a girl or woman becomes another experience added to their painful memories.

Succumbing to the need to be attractive to someone, the desire to become more female than male, dominates their life. They are finding love and acceptance among each other. Who can blame them? We all need love and acceptance and we all must have sex. *We must all have sex.* Gratification will be achieved or at the very least sought after and pursued repeatedly in the direction of the least resistance.

Homophobes are as troubled as homosexuals. A morbid fear of homosexuality can be a consuming tormenting state of spiritual and sexual discord; many times leading to violence towards anyone who is perceived as a threat to their uncompromising heterosexual mindset. The fear of being accused of being a "fag" or approached by a homosexual can result in the brutal battering of the offender in an effort to prove one's heterosexuality.

Ironically, the consequence of the violence often leads to a prison sentence, sometimes for life and the result is a life of homosexuality; the very problem that put him there in the first place. This is sad, isn't it? In an effort to convince the world "I am not a fag," the only sex ever available to him for the rest of his life will be only with another man.

Lesbians too, are searching for gratification. Circumstances and experiences that lead to this choice of lifestyle are encounters with males that have been traumatic and/or completely disappointing. Violent abusive sexual encounters leave them completely void of affection for males. Sexual encounters that have repeatedly proven to be completely one sided pleasure for the man has instilled the feeling of never being able to experience the real joy of sex.

Whatever individual experiences drive people to do what they do as sexual beings, we must learn tolerance because we have never been given even footing in this arena. The deck has been stacked against us and we have never been told of this manipulation. It never should have happened to us, but it did, and we deserve to know the truth of our situation. We have been condemned to live "fixed" lives.

Chapter

A Nurse's Observations

I am a nurse. I studied and completed licensure require-
ments as a Licensed Practical Nurse in the State of Florida.
I have been practicing for 12 years. I do not consider my
specific course of study or career choice as a basis of
authority on the subject discussed in this book. My observations of life, love, marriage and sex are the foundation of
my knowledge base. I do have some knowledge of anatomy
and physiology. I am not an "expert."

I have been compelled to write these bits down and do
my best to reach as many people as possible because this
issue is an issue. A subject matter that is occasionally skirted
on various TV shows, given barely a moments notice and
then discarded. The importance of the issue is missed.
There is a definite lack compassion for our infant sons that
so overwhelms me I am moved to tears for their sake. They
have no voice, save their terrified screams and when

exhaustion overcomes them, silence. No one to say I'm sorry, and no one to make this wrong right. These infants need a voice that will speak for them, that is powerful enough to stop the pain before it occurs.

I have no Ph.D.; I am not a doctor of psychology. I am not a Rhodes Scholar or even a college graduate but having learned this one truth in my life, I will have managed to surpass all of the academic accomplishments of one who is a Ph.D. but refuses to grasp the magnitude of this brutality.

I am a human being with a heart. I am dedicated to "do no harm" professionally as well as personally.

I do this for the babies yet to be born, that face the nightmare that awaits them. If my words can impact one parent who has the backbone to stand on these convictions and one little boy sleeps easy, then I have succeeded.

Our children are taught in school to follow their dreams. They believe they can change the world for the better if they desire. Creativity and individualism is a mainstay of our society. We want it to be. And so we must take a stance to prevent any hardship that is preventable from ever spoiling our children's sense of self worth. This must apply to little boys as it does to little girls.

Suppose what I'm telling you is wrong, about the psychological trauma being permanent, you still have nothing to lose by **not** circumcising your baby boy. He will do just fine as an intact person. If God or nature had truly been flawed then the foreskin would not appear on every little baby boy born. Yet it continues to come as standard equipment on each new model produced. It must serve some function to warrant being there.

If I am right, and you can agree, we may be on track toward a happier world, and healing many of society's ills.

Chapter 12
A Mother's Prayer

If we love our kids, and I mean really love our kids, this small sacrifice of power over them, males especially, but females too, can be an easy choice. Look in your newborn's eyes and say the golden rule to yourself. Do unto others, as you would have them do unto you. Imagine yourself in his diapers and ask yourself if you really need or want to do this to him. Or should I let him sleep and rest easy in my arms, safe from any harm, real or imagined. I know he must be tired, for being born is a stressful thing. He is in my arms perfect and peaceful.

At this moment, do I really want to do the unspeakable to him? Have him stripped and exposed, tied to a board, his tiny arms and legs restrained. Should I allow strangers to touch his most private part, to hurt him there? How would he react? How would he process this pain?

He is so beautiful, peaceful and calm; a gift from God and I believe he is perfect. I do believe this baby is the image of God. Innocent and wise, a being that will change my life. I am happy because of this little boy, and I will swear to protect him with the fierceness of a mother. Nowhere else in nature would a mother allow harm to her young. In fact, when necessary, a mother will place herself in danger in order to protect the cubs, pups, kits, etc. facing down pain or death for the survival and safety of her brood.

I want to be that brave. I want to learn how to be strong enough to do the right thing for my child. It is in my power to start right now. I was happy to be carrying this baby. I took care of myself and I accept the sacrifices and changes I am going to have to face. I am capable of making the right decisions now too.

I want my baby to grow strong and happy. I don't want to worry if he is tormented by a deed that I permitted and refused to stop. I think and I believe that he will live a full life without the painful memory, without the pain that this procedure inflicts.

I will be willing to give him proper instruction about his body. I will seek proper medical care when he really needs it. I will take no unnecessary chances with his body or soul, for I have no right to. I am aware of his boundaries, and I respect his body as I do my own, and I will not succumb to the pressure around me to do what I don't believe in.

I swear to uphold my promise of protection and love. I will strive to instill a sense of love and compassion that will not be thwarted by pain and suffering.

My message of love will be clear and consistent. He will not hear love and feel pain. I will do my part to enable him to achieve his goals. I will encourage him to reach beyond and dream of greatness if he wants to. I will root him in reality and endeavor to preserve his childhood fascination with fantasy and fable. His lust for life and exploration of his world I will guide, but not hinder to the point of squelching his need for independence.

He will be a man one day and the man he becomes will be the result of the choices I make now. I want him to be independent, capable of standing on his own with confidence and self worth.

I cannot promise him a charmed life. I know he will feel pain, be sick, and have girl trouble. I want him to fall in love. I don't expect thanks for allowing him to keep what is his to begin with.

I know I can't give him everything he wants, but I will see that he is fed, clothed and sheltered from the elements. He will be able to count on my support. He will know that I will be there somewhere nearby but not dictating his every move. He will be his own man.

I feel pride and happiness, and he hasn't even been able to look at my face yet. I know he knows me. I know he trusts me. I will not carelessly violate his trust. His faith in me will be founded in the continued comfort and protection I provide for him.

I may not live up to my ideal mother image, yet in making this decision to have and keep my baby, I am obligated to give this my best effort. After all, what more important thing can I do in this life? What will be my legacy to the human race? My contribution should be benevolent and my children are the mark I leave behind.

Chapter 13

Message From My Higher Power

Children, rest easy, I am here.

I love you and I do care about you. I am aware of your suffering too. I created you in my image. My word is very clear on this. You need to trust in my ability to know what is right for you and there is no part of my image that is flawed. Your quest to improve upon perfection has failed miserably and the time to admit this to yourselves and to each other is now. Take a closer look at what I have given to you and rejoice in your flesh. Do not cause harm to come to my gifts to you. I am all knowing and your early vessels are as perfect as I had intended them to be. My love does not require your pain or sacrifice. Never has and never will. Peace to those who have suffered.

* * * * * * * * * *

God's word of love is real. We have made a mockery of him by presuming to know that in this one particular area, God was wrong. God made a mistake, and we being smarter than God have devised a way to improve upon his creation. We have decided that at some point in his divine plan for us he became distracted, lost track of what he was doing, and OOPS! Placed this little fold of skin at the end of the baby boys' penis, and had he been paying closer attention, this would not have happened. Since we have a more careful eye than God does, we have taken it upon ourselves to correct this error.

Personally, if I were to look for flaws in creation I might have questioned the reason why he made some people right handed. That to me is a greater mystery, but one I must live with anyhow. If I can live with that, than I can live with man in his image too.

We have no earthly or spiritual right to second guess our construction, or presume that the body of man is defective. We count fingers and toes, and we hope and pray our babies will be physically normal. Yet when presented with normal, we are somehow compelled to re-manufacture, to alter the original design to suit some other ideation of normal. Explain this.

Chapter
Legally Speaking

We are caught in a quagmire of liability issues.

Most men at this time would not consider legal action against the hospitals and doctors that encouraged and performed infant penile reduction surgeries(PRS). I suspect this is true because most men consider themselves no worse off because of this, and have been told so convincingly that they are in fact better because of this. The attitude of gratitude is incredibly misplaced. Men owe no debt of gratitude for this and if they desire to seek legal counsel to obtain monetary compensation from their loss, the legal and medical communities have a moral obligation to make this as easy as possible for them. They that consider themselves "damaged goods" should be allowed to be heard and if possible, confront the attacker.

They have suffered great pain physically and psychologi-cally. They bear a scar from a procedure that they were in no way capable of consenting to. The suffering should be recognized for what it is and what it is perceived to be by the victim.

In all other situations of malpractice, the public is encouraged to seek the advice of an attorney. At the very least to find out what their rights are under the law and what if anything can be done to compensate in a case of violation.

We have talked to many attorneys in Florida. Not one was willing to discuss the issue any further when they learned that the injury resulted from penile reduction surgery at birth. We received arguments regarding statute of limitations and that his parents should have considered seeking damages in the first years of his life.

However, his parents were never informed of the accident and never knew that their child nearly died because of this. Doctors did not come right out and tell them that their baby had suffered cruel and unusual treatment at the hands of a so-called competent practitioner. Mother believed the trauma was minimal and that nothing was askew with Jerry's PRS. If she did, she used shock and denial as defense mechanisms in order not to face the fact that her baby boy was now deformed for life.

Of course, the climate of the times discouraged lay people from questioning the all-knowing medical community and if they said nothing was wrong, then the subject was closed. They were not wasting any more of their valuable time answering stupid questions from stupid people. Besides, there were hundreds of baby boys that needed circumcision and time was of the essence. (Mustn't let the baby go home, lest the parent should decide against it later. And no one was to escape). All baby boys were suffering from quality-of- life-threatening conditions from which modern medicine was on a crusade to stamp out.

The practice of PRS in infancy has become so much a part of society now, those attempting to receive compensation are laughed at and trivialized. Men have enough trouble accepting the laughter in all other aspects of their lives especially the laughter of women, that it is necessary that someone assume the responsibility to recognize the pain, empathize, and at least, try to take someone seriously when they call on them for help. Humiliation is no way to treat someone in pain, yet society does this daily and laughter from doctors and lawyers is nearly as barbaric as the act itself.

Lawyers, if you receive a call from a man or his wife, you can bet that they have borne the very last straw, and that public disclosure of their plight may lead to further hurt. Listen and convey a sense of compassion. This will be very helpful even if legal recourse is not possible. We are all very fragile.

Examine your own experiences. We all have demons. What are yours? Do you reject the possibilities because of some terrible loss of your own? These babies are helpless and hunted. They cannot speak for themselves and they deserve a voice passionate for their cause. Do you have the courage to defeat the beast, and insure that babies have a voice?

Stand with me for the sake of the innocent. Protect them in infancy and until they are of age to make decisions for themselves based on knowledge and experience and full disclosure. Thank you.

Chapter

A Letter To Men

I understand that these concepts are going to be very difficult to accept. You will be reluctant to sway your belief that
this procedure was beneficial and necessary. It had no bear-
ing on your existence as a man and you stand fast on this.
This is a natural and expected response.

I want you to know that I admire you, all of you. I am
awed by the very maleness of your gender and it is my pleasure to know you. Not on a personal level, of course, but all
of you share a common quality that I find irresistible. Thank
God! I mean for both of us.

I will once more with all my heart implore you to take
heed of these humble words. Do not harm yourselves, or
your sons. Your greatness and my admiration for you are at
stake. When I ponder the great things that man has done, I
cannot help to puzzle over the question of cleanliness. Is it
really possible that men can launch one another into earth's

orbit, annihilate smallpox from the face of the earth, harness nuclear power, dive three miles below the surface of the ocean and yet cannot be entrusted with his own hygiene? I ask myself how is this possible. In 6,000 years of recorded history and forward progress, this is an area of severe concern, for you to be subjected to a surgical solution. How can I accept that? How can you?

If you do, then I must. For I hold you accountable for your decision, as you must also accept accountability for any error in judgment. Remember. Remember your brothers as well, for you all share a common experience that binds you into brotherhood. Welcome this feeling of unity. You can gain strength from each other, and you need strength.

You are not at fault for what happened to you. You are not to blame, for your bodies are what they were manufactured to be. Not by your choice, but by someone else's. Take special care to control your outrage. Anger will be even more destructive.

Do not allow this to continue. Stop the routine circumcision of infant males today.

Your protection of the innocent will be your compensation and solace. I back you 100%. Look to Kubler-Ross for understanding grief.

A Letter to Woman

Love and respect your men. They may be hard to understand and even more difficult to tolerate. We are moved toward them by a power greater than ourselves and if we fight this, war against it even, we risk losing a part of ourselves. Men are good for us. I understand that we are confused as to why, but trust me they are.

We must be willing to go one step further and recognize the error of our judgment: that our actions, no matter how benign they appear to be at the time, can and do have dire consequences. That in damaging our men, we have damaged ourselves. Are we really willing to continue this, to repeat the cycle in an attempt to absolve ourselves from the past?

Allow the cycle to be broken. Insist that it be broken. Give yourselves a chance to know a natural man at some point in your life. When you are old and your full-grown son looks into your eyes let him see your pride in him. Do not let this warm moment be clouded by a specter of guilt. He will love you and protect you, as you did for him. This is the natural course. Allow yourself to enjoy this moment for this is the purpose of life. Our future rests in the hearts of our children. Give them what their fathers never had a chance for. This is your reward.

Do not be content to internalize sexual dysfunction. We are not to blame either physically or psychologically. We do not need to pursue sensuality through self-incrimination. Makeup, perfume, and sexy lingerie are fun and alluring, but don't expect miracles from these.

Be willing to admit that our men have been subjected to Penile Reduction Surgery, and that they could do nothing to prevent this. Our sex lives are what they are by human design. Not what we expected, a hand we were dealt and are forced to play.

Maintain your dignity and do not fail your man for it is not his desire to fail you. Listen with your hearts.

Chapter

Experience, the Best Teacher
(Life's Credentials)

10

I'm sure that in order to prove credibility I am going to have to share personal experience. I don't mind doing this.

I became sexually active at a very early age. I was aware of my ability to achieve an orgasm from masturbation when I was very young. This is not earth shattering news, as I am sure that many women can relate to this. I liked it, and I did this often. Masturbation was always followed a deep sense of guilt. I felt like a law-breaker, and I can't say for sure why I had this feeling. It seemed wrong. Perhaps the Victorian attitudes of sex and sin still permeated our lives. SEX is SIN.

I began having sexual intercourse when I was about fourteen. I expected that sex with a man would be good as well. I am not sure what I expected, but I was repeatedly disappointed by sex. The guys seemed to be enjoying sex a lot more than I was. Soon I began to believe that this was the way intercourse was supposed to be, one-sided pleasure, purely for the benefit of the male.

I sought pleasure frequently, changing partners often, hoping for the magic. The search was futile. Something was wrong with me. I had the desire, I had the capability. I was sure that there must be a defect with my own physiology. Perhaps I did not possess the "G-spot" that I had read about. I formed my own responses and beliefs about sex.

Guys were easily excited by my feigned orgasms during intercourse, and quickly finished the act, prompted by my displays. Sex soon became a series of quickies, not the extreme pleasurable experiences I was expecting. I became disillusioned with sex very soon. This was a man's domain, his pleasure palace. Not intended for women to enjoy. Yet in my heart I could not fully accept this. There must be more to sex than procreation.

Since men enjoyed sex so much, and I enjoyed the company of men, I continued to participate. Resigned to the role of pleasure giver and the receiver of essentially nothing, as far as intercourse was concerned. Clitoral orgasms were the central part of my sexual pleasure. Even though I was having plenty of sex, I was not having plenty of fun. Faking pleasure during intercourse became standard operating procedure. A good fake can certainly bring a guy to climax much quicker than expressing the true disdain and indifference that I felt. Many partners went away thinking they were the monster fuck of my life. So sad to tell you guys who may be reading this that I am not alone in this deception. There are many women who do this. You can't tell if they don't want you to know. This is not because we want to feel like this. We did not make a conscious choice to dislike sex.

We have been handed this cup of poison and forced to drink.

A little later, I chanced upon an encounter that would forever alter my perspective and attitudes. I met a natural man: an intact man. At the ripe old age of seventeen, I was jaded, and convinced that there was nothing about sex that I did not already know. No male could do the magic for me. Yet I was still young and full of sexual energy, so I had not given up completely. I let this man come into my life.

I was amazed by his size. He was very different from the previous lovers I had been with. I liked him too. I believe that my feelings for him impacted our passion deeply. I did not want to seem too impressed with his natural endowments, but there was no denying, that in all my personal encounters, I had never met any one that compared.

He had a gentle power, and a sense of self-confidence that was also new to me. He was in no rush to do the deed. In fact he was hesitant. I knew that he wanted to, but was not nearly as pressured as the others. This calmness, and self-control, was especially exciting. What was he holding back from me? What was his special gift? It was, for the first time in my life, my own eagerness to find out these things that brought us together intimately. Our first time together was not an incredible experience, at that moment. My first awareness that he had touched me in a very different way actually came the next morning when I first sat up. I was in some distress, my abdomen hurt. This had never happened before. The soreness was similar to that the day after you begin a work out of sit-ups. I was worried that he had done some damage.

He visited me early that day and seemed not at all surprised at my condition. He was concerned for me though, and explained that it was normal for me to be uncomfortable. His remedy, as you might guess, was to get right back in the saddle. Which he/we did. I had no difficulty. I expected extreme discomfort, but was pleasantly surprised to realize how good this was for me. We fit naturally together, I experienced no pain, no soreness internally, and no eagerness for him to climax.

Sex is sublime. Natural sexual intercourse, that is natural sex as it is intended, between natural people, untouched by human surgical intervention, is exactly what we envision it to be. Extremely sensual, and extremely pleasurable. It is actually a mutually participatory activity. I was an active partner for the first time. My body came alive in his embrace, and I was able to direct the course of our lovemaking, and share the experience of orgasm with my lover. We could easily anticipate the need and desire of each other, every fiber of our physical selves melted together as one, and we never miss-fired. Lovemaking can last for hours. Without losing grip or stamina. Energy is shared, and stamina renewed by the sincere desire to bring each other to new heights. The natural larger than average size of an intact penis makes staying connected much easier, and manual manipulation of the prepuce internally is extremely pleasurable. We could lie perfectly still, not moving a muscle outwardly, and yet the action inside was intense. I found that the most comfortable sleep I ever had was sleeping with this man still inside me. A slight movement could easily bring us both to full awareness and often we would resume, well rested, and eager to begin again. The sensations were so intense, so sensual that having to stop was the most discomforting, and saddest of times. Imagine lovemaking so sweet that you weep from the happiness that this kind of pleasure brings you.

This has become rare and often never experienced by most of us. Circumcision permanently alters the male and prohibits him from ever being able to give as well as receive this kind of sexual pleasure. This is the intended outcome of neonatal circumcision. It is a punishment, inflicted initially on the male and ultimately on both men and women when they reach the age of sexual maturity. Infant circumcision diminishes the size of the adult penis by interfering with and retarding the natural growth and development of the penis. This diminished size inhibits the man from reaching deep inside the vagina, and finding that spot. You must remember that our bodies are capable of great stretching and great conformity. Nature would not have given us parts incapable of receiving her bounty. The loss of the prepuce causes an increase in friction, which results in abraisions occurring on the vaginal walls. This soreness is usually attributed to the lack of female lubrication, and so unsatisfactory intercourse is blamed on the woman. The foreskin acts as a protective, lubricating barrier inside the vagina. This enables a smoother, natural glide, that eliminates the need for artificial jellies.

We dated for several months. Each encounter was nothing less than spectacular. He never asked "was it good for you?" This inquiry was unnecessary. He knew by my sincerity and genuine responses to him that I was enjoying myself immensely. There was no need for deception, and certainly no room for feigned ecstasy. This was the real thing! This is what we, as human beings, were born to experience with one another. Natural men making love with natural women. It is the soul of our existence. It is the divine plan for us to be in harmony sexually, and we are made in a specific way to insure this.

I was invited to Eden and I went. I stayed long enough to learn the truth, and then was uninvited just as abruptly. I regret my visit, because I will never be able to forget it. This memory and the knowledge it imparts to me, will curse me to my grave. I know how my life has been corrupted by the fear that drives men to do such horrific deeds to one another. There is no greater loss than the loss of the pure and natural. This is our birthright, and it has been stolen from us. Men and women have been robbed of their true selves, and been repaid with lies.

Many do not understand the true nature of their loss. This is another aspect of the perfect crime. If you never had something, there is no way of really knowing how much you miss it. Understanding the basic concept of natural compatibility will bring you closer to the realization. Admitting that there is a real, definite reason for us to be made the way we are is the path to enlightenment.

✳   ✳   ✳   ✳   ✳   ✳   ✳   ✳   ✳   ✳

I have been married to Jerry for a long time. We have managed to stay faithful to one another. We have had full knowledge of these truths for years, and we have shared our understanding with our family, friends, and occasionally coworkers. Often the response is complete denial and a steadfast refusal to even consider that this little operation is the destroyer of our sex, and that the sabotage of our sex has led to the breakdown of our intimate relationships, and has brought discord and turmoil into our personal lives. The denial is so strong, because the truth is so painful. Denial is the survival mechanism, an absolute necessity to insure the continuation of one's peace of mind. We have used it ourselves. There are many times that denial has been comforting, but only for a little while, then the truth comes flooding in. I honestly believe that when all else fails, our bodies, our minds, our memory, this one truth will remain. We have even joked that not even a lobotomy would be able to take this from us. With our luck we would lose everything else, and the truth of circumcision would remain.

When you know something, you know it in your bones. You know also that everyone else knows, but the will to survive accepts this altered state and even calls it normal. To prove it we allow, and even insist that we do this to those we love in a show that displays we **can** do this to someone and love is no less. The truth is very close though, just under the surface, and it takes great resolve to face it. The truth is devastating. The act is permanent, irreversible. The pain is real, and so is the blood and screaming. It is time that we accept circumcision as the destructive curse that it is, and work to silence the screams of the innocents forever. Put an end to this brutality, and once and for all say no to this damning practice that has touched us in our infancy and reached far into the future to invade our bedrooms. It can be stopped one infant boy at a time. But the power to do this rests in the hearts and hands of the parents. Mothers and fathers turn your hearts to your children.

Fathers, you must say, "I do not want my son to be like me in this way. I want him to be as he was created, better off than I am. I want my son to be safe and happy. I want him to be a natural man". You have the strength to do this one thing. This will be the most important decision you can make for your boy. It is in your power. Sadly it is in your power to give your son what is already his, and what you were never given-options. You had no choice. The decision was made for you, and while you may believe this is A-okay with you, it is still your body and someone else made the decision to painfully alter your genitals. It was a violation, it was an abuse of power. And you have to live every day of your life with the mark of this decision on your penis. Ask yourselves honestly. 'Do I really need for my son to be like me?' Is there even a remote possibility that nature made him perfect already?' 'Can I accept perfection?' 'Can I love my son unconditionally, or do I have to insist he bear a similar, or perhaps a worse disfigurement that I do?'

Circumcision can be performed later in life. Rest assured that if your son chooses to have this done when he is a man, and reached the age of consent, that he will be anesthetized, and proper care will be taken of him. He will be fully aware of his options. I doubt that he will choose this for himself though. I am certain that he will be contented with his body and the notion of cutting on his penis will be foreign and downright perverted to him.

Give him the chance. It is a basic human right we all cherish-to have dominion over our own bodies. Women have struggled for this right for ourselves, and loss of control over our own bodies is a foe for both genders to unite against. Don't take your son's choice from him. If you do, he will not thank you for it when he learns the truth of your actions. We will all suffer further indignity and loss of personal freedom if we don't begin to look out for one another now.

Can you bear to hear him say to you, 'how could you let this happen to me? I did not ask for this!'

Chapter

Restoration?

It is very important that I mention this, and include in this book, information about restoration and my opinions related to this. I have learned by researching foreskin restoration this is certainly possible, and desirable. Throughout history foreskin restoration has been accomplished successfully. Men that have been circumcised have regained coverage of the glans by a dedicated commitment to a program of stretching the remaining skin. Resulting in a more natural looking, and natural feeling penis.

In times of persecution, circumcising cultures have used foreskin restoration as a means of blending, and disguising their heritage to avoid slaughter. In these modern times, men who have become aware of the harmful effects of circumcision regain a sense of self-ownership and control, through restoration. They are committed to success and achieve success, through determination, and support from other men that are restoring.

This requires first, that a man recognize that a beautiful and sacred part of him was wrongfully taken. That this part of him **is** important, and worth having. Facing the reality that a man's body is just as worthy and just as sacred as a woman's. And setting aside the lie that it is not.

Our society has erroneously proclaimed that a man's body, and his personal right to wholeness is not worthy of consideration at all. 'Its' dirty, its' just extra skin, it smells, its' infectious, and finally, its' not even his for chris-sakes'. The decision to alter rests solely on the whim, preference, and most often, the ignorance of the parent. We do not condone or even consider likewise alteration of the female infants' body. In fact, this would be, and is, interpreted as abuse and mutilation. This is **wrong**. This inequitable protection and consideration must be brought to a halt now. This is sexual discrimination at its' very worse.

Recognizing this violation will be absolutely necessary before a successful program of restoration can begin. A man must know that what happened to him, can not be allowed to continue to happen to others. Saving himself requires that he be willing to save and inform others. For one can not embark on a journey to freedom, without contributing to secure freedom for others.

Compare foreskin restoration to mastectomy recovery. You will have to reach in order to do this, because they are fundamentally different. In contrast, a mastectomy survivor understands that her loss was the result of a life-saving procedure. She would have no hope of survival without the sacrifice of her breast. Is she mutilated? Yes. Is she psychologically harmed? Yes. She feels less of a woman, because she has lost one, or perhaps both of her breasts. Does she want to look normal again? Yes. Has a man lost his foreskin, a part of his natural penis, as a life-saving measure? No. He has lost this body part because of a social stigma. His life, or health was not in jeopardy. Yet he was painfully subjected to an amputation of a portion of his body he holds just as dear. His foreskin does not offend, or threaten him in any way. Foreskin restoration is comparable to the desire of a woman seeking prosthetic replacement of her breasts following a medical amputation. It is completely normal, and completely desirable to want to consider foreskin restoration.

The absolute plus side to foreskin restoration is the functionality of the end result. While breast prosthesis are very meaningful to the psychological well-being of the woman, they are not physically functional. A new foreskin actually works in the manner nature intended. It provides coverage and increased sensitivity to the glans, which promotes the recovery of more natural sensory reception. During sexual intercourse, the foreskin functions to reduce friction and irritation to both surfaces of the vagina and the penis. This results in a more comfortable, enjoyable, sexual experience.

Sometimes during the separation of the glans and foreskin in infant circumcision, the glans is damaged. Tearing and scarring result. This can affect sensation of the glans for the rest of the persons' life. Foreskin restoration can not correct this. But this should not be considered a reason to not attempt restoration. Improvement is possible. Testimonials, from the men that I have read on the internet, substantiate this. The damage from circumcision can often include the total or partial excision of the frenulum, frenar band, and ridged bands. These are highly sensitive, erogenous structures. If they have been excised or damaged, this also, can not be corrected by restoration.

Benefits include some increase in the length and girth. Circumcision at birth interferes with the normal growth and development of the penis. Limiting the over-all size of the adult member. As I stated earlier I hardly believe there are men who would actually prefer a smaller penis. Self-worth, and esteem are the most significant beneficial outcomes. A realization, that as a male you do have value as a physical being.

Detailed information concerning foreskin restoration, including techniques, support groups, and testimonials from men that are restoring are available at various websites. These websites also offer extensive access to may links on the subject. Much information is at your disposal for perusal. I will list the sites, and organizations that are going to be very helpful later in this chapter. I suggest that if you are interested in learning more about the subject of restoration, that you visit these sites. The hosts are very amicable and willing to offer help and referrals, relating to this facet of circumcision.

You may also feel the need to consult with your physician before beginning a program of restoration. I fully understand this, especially if you are experiencing sexual difficulty. I have to caution you though, you may not, and likely will not, receive much support from this venue. Remember that routine infant circumcision is a mainstay of modern medicine. It receives much support from the medical community, and the idea of wanting to restore, the part that they are responsible for taking, is going to set uneasily with them. Prepare yourself first, by visiting the web-sites and educating yourself as much as you can. You become the authority, knowledge is a powerful thing, and so is hope. Do not allow your doctor to dash both. For a physician to encourage and understand one's desire for this, he must be willing to recognize that the loss of the foreskin is not the desirable state they have been telling us it is for all our lives. It is the medical profession of this country that brought this upon us, and the medical profession is not going to change its' position on this any time soon. They have become deeply entrenched proponents of circumcision for many reasons, and will not forsake this stance easily. Millions of American men have been circumcised in the last hundred years, based on the advice of the collective majority of physicians. What will happen to the overall structure of the medical system if it is fully recognized, and held accountable as the thief of our sex?

The demigods will fall and the admission of a terrible mistake will bring down the temple.

So be wary when seeking the advice or support from your doctor. You will likely be scoffed at, and possibly humiliated or shamed into feeling that your concern for your intimate body and sexuality is perverted or unmanly. This is some of the arsenal used to keep the practice alive and thriving. Counting on the surmise that men will be shamed into silence easily, quickly and completely.

Recently it was reported that medical mistakes are the eighth leading cause of death. This has provoked a call for mandatory reporting of errors to federal authorities. This proposal was overwhelmingly decried by the medical establishment. They do not want to have to report all errors, and prefer the current practice of handling problems within the system, remain as it is. The covert rationale for this is to keep public knowledge regarding errors at a minimum. This includes millions of botched circumcisions performed by unskilled surgical novices and even seasoned practitioners that have regarded the procedure as **minor**, and not worthy of their full attention. In fact many surgeons consider the procedure not significant enough for them to waste their time on, and then delegate this job to underlings. This procedure has been minimized to the degree of comparing it to ear piercing. I say, when women begin having sex with their earlobes, then we can compare practices. The attitude of triviality has resulted in inconsistent training and education, and poor to disgraceful outcomes for millions of men. These *botched jobs* have not been reported, and documented in an ethical manner, ever. Forced disclosure will surely mean an end to the practice.

Even today, when presented with a poor result of circumcision, doctors will respond with a smug, 'oh, thats' nothing, you can still have kids'. This is the voice of personal experience. It is sad and tragic. So if you feel you must consult with a physician with a problem that may interfere with your program of restoration, seek one that is sympathetic, and understanding. Ask specific questions, and be alert for any sign of not being taken seriously. Consult the web. Many of your questions and concerns may be expounded upon by someone who has already walked the same road ahead of you.

Whatever you decide to do, whether it be restoration or not, the support you receive from these various resources will be invaluable to obtaining a greater understanding of what happened to you. The reasons for why it was done are not going to be acceptable at all, and that is the most difficult thing to live with. Having someone to talk to, and express your true feelings to about this, is essential. I strongly urge all wives, girlfriends, and parents to open your minds and your hearts to the ones you love. We have all lost in this bargain of our sex for money, and we must all share in the recovery of our spirit that was also sacrificed in this dirty deal. If the man you love decides he will begin to restore, it is your obligation to him to be supportive, understanding, and helpful. Patients and perserverence are the key to success. The sense of regaining some control over one's body is the greatest reward, and long overdue for most of us. We have spent our whole lives on the receiving end of endless jokes, ridicule, and embarrassment, leaving us confused and hurting inside, trying with all we have to be and act like sexually whole, and fully functional individuals, which we are not. Now we have tools, the knowledge, and understanding, to do what is in our power to correct as much of the damage as possible. Unity and compassion will see us through this, and spare future generations from enduring the same fate we have faced down. We are truly on the edge of becoming a generation that does care for one another, and love is not a word we just used to flash on posters, and lost complete site of as we aged. We can get it back.

Resources

NOCIRC
PO Box 2512
San Anselmo,Ca. 94979-2512
U.S.A.
415-488-9883
Web address: www.nocirc.org

Circumcision Resource Center
Ronald Goldman Ph.D.
PO Box 232
Boston, MA. 02133
e-mail: crc@ziplink.net

Doctors Opposing Circumcision
2442 NW Market St. #42
Seattle, WA. 98107
206-368-9428
e-mail: gcd@uwashington.edu

National Organization of Restoring Men
(NORM)
R. Wayne Griffiths, M.S.
3205 Northwood Drive #209
Concord CA. 94520-4506
510-827-4119
e-mail: waynerobb@aol.com

National Organization to Halt the Abuse and
Routine Mutilation of Males (NOHARMM)
Activist Organization for Men
Tim Hammond
PO Box 460795
San Francisco, CA 94146
415-826-9351
e-mail: info@noharmm.org

Epilogue

We have been told all of our lives that the size of a man's penis has nothing to do with our capability of enjoying sex. We have trusted these words and so have been in turmoil with ourselves as to why we do not enjoy sex. There must be something wrong with us. If we desire better sex, we are whorish or somehow bad. We must never entertain the thought that dissatisfaction with sex has anything to do with our men.

I ask you, does this really seem fair? Is it right that we reproach ourselves so vehemently? Deny flatly that there could be anything amiss with man's physiology and performance? We are after all natural women. We have not endured any manmade intervention on our bodies. Why then this dissatisfaction? Are we somehow mentally or emotionally defective?

The answer lies in the practice of routine infant circumcision. Our men have been altered in infancy through penile reduction surgery. They are unnatural men trying to pleasure natural women. The sexual dysfunction of our generation is the direct result of the mutilation of our men that occurred when they were barely days old. The removal of their foreskin forever changed their ability to give women orgasms during sexual intercourse. Intercourse is for male stimulation and procreation only. Women have been excluded forever from receiving orgasm during copulation, and men have been sentenced to experience only a limited measure of pleasure. This is the design and purpose of circumcision.

Our parents were never told this, though perhaps if they had been, there would have been far fewer of these procedures performed. Even if you believe that the procedure has in no way been detrimental, you must ask yourself, how can natural and unnatural find harmony? This is a question of basic common sense. The two will experience dysfunction and discord. It is the only possible result.

We have to be smarter about our sexuality and must insist that our sex organs be left intact as nature intended. If we don't insist on sanity in this one aspect of nature, how can we possibly expect future generations to respect our planet? How can we tell ourselves and our children, that nature is to be respected and preserved when we continue to disrespect and disregard our most prized natural resource—ourselves?

Rest assured, our children are going to be acutely tuned in to this discrepancy and our hypocrisy will be evident. Respect for our insistence that they practice conservation and environmental protection will fly in our faces if we continue to practice sexual mutilation on their small and defenseless bodies. We are on track for disaster. In fact, we are already enmeshed in disaster, but have yet to recognize this.

I am calling for national awareness of our most egregious error and rally all to the cause of the protection of children. Protection that we ourselves were denied, but still owe to our children and grandchildren.

I may be shouting to the wind, my words may easily fall on deaf ears, and I will be of no consequence in helping the human race save itself. Yes, I believe that our survival as a quality species is in danger of being lost forever. That our hope lies in the humane treatment of our infant sons, for the benefit of the peace of mind and confidence that comes from knowing he is just as nature and God intended him to be.

Do not waste this opportunity. Make a real difference in your loved ones lives. Prove that you really do love him and will not be tempted to corrupt his sex for any reason.

I will close this little book now. Not because I have nothing else to say, or because I feel I have managed to convince you, but because this is much to assimilate, and some may have great difficulty with these words. The trauma that I experienced and have lived with is no easy thing to bear. Life has been hard for me, knowing these things and having no recourse, no possible way to go back and fix it. And no one to express this to. To the rest of the world this is a matter of no significance. That I am not able to accept the lies and be comfortable with this situation was only my personal mental illness. If I could but believe what I have been told, then I would share in this restless slumber.

Reader, you decide. Be cautious though, for your decision will impact lives long after you are dead. Allow your descendants to remember you well -that you were a child in bondage and through your strength you were able to lead your people to freedom from this thing that plagued your ancestors. That circumcision of infant males was a monumental failure and reason and sanity presided because of your resolve.

Go with God.

Lisa

Correspondence

Letter to the Editor, Lake City Reporter
8/27/99
From: Lisa Bisque

Circumcision is child abuse

I am writing this letter to focus attention on an appalling medical practice that is hurting our children. We have been told for years that circumcision is harmless and beneficial, that it is necessary to prevent problems that may occur later in life and that it will insure social acceptance. We have been lied to.

The procedure is extremely painful. The infant is helpless to stop this from happening to him. He would if he could. He is restrained with Velcro fasteners on a board that must be bolted to a table so that he does not buck himself and the board onto the floor. His tiny body is then subjected to the harsh treatment of cold steel , scissors, clamps, and even fingernails are used to do the amputation. This is amputation of a perfectly designed and functional body part. Every baby that endures this cries. Cries so desperate that this alone should have ended the practice years ago. Yet the cries of agony are repeatedly ignored.

The loss that this procedure induces has been minimized, so that people will continue to do this to their babies. The amputation of the infant's foreskin results in the loss of about 50 percent of the adult's penis. Fifteen square inches. This loss is very significant. The loss of erogenous tissue is significant. Nerves are cut and blood supply is interrupted. Over time, the loss of the protective sheath Leaves the glans dry and desensitized. This results in abnormal sexual experience for both partners.

The physical scar of circumcision is life-long. The victim is forever marked by this act. This is a medical intervention that the person never consented to. The baby has had no opportunity to reject this. This lack of consent is a violation of an individual's right to choose what he wants for himself. Can we truly call ourselves a democracy? Right now, our future leaders and citizens are being surgically altered sexually, by force.

This is not freedom. This is another form of slavery. People with heart and vision must work to stop this. Circumcision is child abuse.

Circumcision Has Health Benefits

Regarding newborn circumcision: Your readers should be aware of a more balanced opinion on this very frequent operation. In my office, the procedure is done with local anesthesia. Pain is kept to a minimum.

There are different ways of doing the operation. I prefer to use a device that minimizes the cutting of tissue and yet yields a consistently excellent result. The baby often falls asleep during the procedure. A small amount of (5 percent of penile skin) tissue is removed., with all of the erectile tissue and head of the penis left untouched. There is no residual scar. For adult men that have the operation, sexual performance is almost always improved. Their partners especially appreciate the improved hygiene.

There are proven medical benefits such as better penile hygiene, lower rate of urine infections and reduced incidence of penile cancer. Circumcision is required for a child suffering from a pinhole opening in the foreskin.

Thank goodness that in our democracy, the public can easily obtain correct information and then make an informed decision regarding this common procedure.

Geoff Lloyd-Smith, M.D., F.R.C.S.
Board certified urologists

No Benefits To Circumcision

Dr. Geoff Lloyd-Smith's letter is full of the myths that have been perpetuating circumcision in America, the only country (except South Korea) that amputates normal foreskin from a majority of its sons without religious reasons.

While he may use local anesthesia, only 25% of obstetricians currently use any. The infant does not fall "asleep." He goes into a coma while "5%" of the penile skin is not removed. The usual amount is close to 50%, and may be greater. In the adult, this represents 12-15 square inches, and includes the ridged bands, which contain most of the erogenous nerve endings. Circumcision is not "required" for a pinhole opening in the foreskin. So long as he can urinate, he is just fine, and time will take care of the small opening.

Last, but hardly least, there are no proven medical benefits, as Dr. Lloyd-Smith alleges. Not a single national medical organization in the entire world approves of routine circumcision. The American Academy of Pediatrics stated in their new policy that alleged "benefits are not sufficient to recommend circumcision." This means that the disadvantage, the harm, is greater. Therefore, there are no longer any medical indications, a point we have been making for years.

If there are no medical indications, what is a doctor doing when he cuts normal body parts from another human being without the permission of that individual? Does his license permit this? Go figure, but meanwhile, parents please realize that the doctors who have been doing this no longer have any support for the practice, and we, along with Dr. Spock, encourage you to "leave your little son's penis alone."

Dr. George C. Denniston
Norland, Washington
President of Doctors Opposing Circucmcision

Benefits of Circumcision Questioned

About 80 percent of men worldwide are uncircumcised. But in the United States, a circumcision is performed every 25 seconds, making it the most common elective surgery.

However the numbers of the country's circumcised—about 60 percent—are decreasing as more people oppose the procedure.

While some doctors insist the procedure is necessary to reduce infections and sexually transmitted diseases, a recent 1999 report by the American Academy of Pediatrics concluded that the medical benefits of circumcision no longer justify its use.

"It is a violation of human rights to force the procedure on a newborn," said nurse Lisa Bisque, who characterized the procedure as child abuse in a recent Letter to the Editor of the *Lake City Reporter.* "If most of the world's men are not being circumcised, then maybe we are doing something wrong."

Ronald Goldman, author of Circumcision: *The Hidden Trauma,* said the United States is the only country in the world that circumcises most male infants for non-religious reasons, according to a recent article in *The Boston Globe.*

But Dr. Geoff Lloyd-Smith, who performs about 30 circumcisions a year on older males in Lake City, dismissed claims that circumcision provides no medical benefits. He said a number of his patients come in for the procedure as a result of chronic infections or phimoses, an abnormal tightening at the end of the foreskin.

"It may not be an evil tissue, but many men do find that it causes problems later on in life," Lloyd-Smith said. He added that a number of infections and problems can result from not being circumcised, including paraphimoses, which occurs when the excess skin is pulled over the penis, tightens up and can't be pulled back causing the head to swell.

"The tightened foreskin can balloon, which will require emergency treatment," he said.

Dr. Edgar Schoen, who oversaw a report that claims circumcision reduces the risks of urinary tract infections and sexually transmitted diseases, rejected the academy's report and labeled it "a step backward," according to *The Globe* Article.

"Its highly biased," said Schoen, director of the perinatal screening program at Kaiser Permanente Medical Center in Oakland Calif. "The AAP report says it is not essential to current well-being. Well 90 percent of what we do is not for well-being."

While circumcision remains popular in the United States, today's 60 percent rate is far from the nearly 90 percent number of the late 1960s. But that drop also may bring the United States closer to the world's penile cancer rate.

Lloyd said while there is little scientific evidence to support that people who have not been circumcised are at risk for penile cancer, the condition does occur more frequently in areas of the world where circumcision is not practiced.

Bisque disagreed with that logic. "To say that circumcision should be performed on newborn males as a prevention for infections or cancer is like performing a mastectomy on newborn girls to prevent breast cancer," she said.

The AAP report says if circumcision is chosen, injections of lidocaine should be used to prevent "pain and psychological stress". Bisque said that the extreme pain during the procedure sometimes causes babies to lose consciousness.

Lloyd confirmed that the tests show disturbing changes in babies' crying, heart-rate and oxygen saturation in the blood during the procedure. Most doctors have started using anesthesia within the last five years.

In a few instances, males have had to become females because of damage that resulted from circumcision surgeries. But Lloyd said that is extremely rare and is the result of incompetent doctors.

Thank you for printing my letter. I am now responding to the reply by Dr. Geoff Lloyd-Smith on July 26.

I wish to point out that the doctor did not address the issue of informed Consent by the patient. This is my primary concern. The freedom of choice is completely denied the infant, who *is* the patient. This is the violation of routine infant circumcision. The infant must endure for a life a decision made by others, based on their opinions concerning *his* health, *his* hygiene, *his* appearance, and *his* sexuality. We live in a society that prizes freedom, and this procedure is a direct contradiction, and does not enhance a person's sense of personal freedom regarding his body.

The opinion of enhanced personal hygiene I find to be most degrading. To insinuate that a modern man is incapable of personal hygiene apart from surgical intervention is insulting. To admit that problems that *may* arise from the sex organ are best dealt with by preventive surgery in infancy is a blow to the confidence we have in our physicians. I am disheartened by the revelation that doctors are not prepared, or willing to preserve the foreskin of our males. Amputation in relation to any other body part is a radical, aggressive, last resort effort to save the life of the patient. Yet, amputation of the infant male's foreskin is considered "routine and minor" and the first offense against *possible* problems.

Regarding the claim of "no residual scar" is absurd. Any surgery, any cutting of the skin, is going to leave a physical scar. Of course some scars are worse than others. A circumcision scar, however, is not one that people display, or boast about, and is hidden by clothing, but that does not mean it isn't there.

I still consider that circumcision is child abuse. I hope that doctors become more willing to give up this most lucrative surgery-and prove their skills at correct diagnoses, conservative treatment of the male's sex organ, and preservation of the foreskin, rather than destruction, become the primary concern.

Lisa Bisque
Lake City

Editor's note: The writer is a Licensed Practical Nurse

John Hagee
P.O. Box 1400
San Antonio, Tx. 78295-1400

Routine Infant Circumcision

This letter is very important to me. My husband and I are listeners and subcsribers. We play your tapes frequently, and have benefited from your ministry tremendously.

We believe as you do, that our nation is dire need of spiritual intervention. We have been deceived by our leaders, and this deception has led to our spiral downward. The greatest deception I believe, is that the routine circumcision of infant boys, is a benign, even beneficial, medical intervention.

The surgical alteration of infant males sex organs has had a severe negative impact on the social, and sexual relationships of the adults that have been subjected to this in infancy. Our bodies were created to interact specifically as they were designed. We are supposed to fit together, and work together. The cutting away of the infant males prepuce has forever altered the natural course of this interaction.

The result of this act is the sexual chaos, and discord, we are witness to, and victims of. There is no other outcome that can be expected. What happens to the male will inevitably affect the female. Cause and effect. A cycle of negativity is created, and the result is the out-of-control sexual behaviors that have become the daily norm in this country.

The bible teaches us, that in marriage, the wife has not power over her body, but the husband, and conversely, the husband has not power over his body, but the wife. Modern medicine has taken the power of our bodies completely away from us. For in the instant that the foreskin is forcibly, removed, the power is in the hands of the parent and the Dr. The mark of sexual ownership is delivered upon the child, and can never be reversed. The parents and the Dr.'s influence follows him into his adulthood, to the most intimate realm of his existence.

This is the lie of the century. Our parents were grossly deceived, and the deception has been passed down through generations. Circumcision is medically, penile reduction surgery. It is the amputation of vital erogenous tissue, that is essential in the mutual sexual fulfillment of men and women.

We have placed ourselves at odds with each other. We are not as our Creator intended us to be, but rather products of an act of terrorism. An attack, perpetrated upon an innocent newborn, whose only act of provocation was to be born male.

I implore you consider this subject seriously. All of our social and sexual issues cannot be solved by the cessation of this practice, but we have a responsibility to protect the genital integrity of future generations. People are beginning to become aware of the significant loss inflicted upon them, and children are better informed they ever were. Exposure of this lie is forthcoming, and many will no doubt, look to their religious and political leaders for answers.

I am certain that God had intended for us to be happy together, as men and women. His design of our bodies was intentional, and all knowing. Our arrogance of second guessing His perfection will, and has cursed us.

Thankyou for your time. We hope that this issue will not be overlooked, or ignored. The right to sexual intactness is universal, and parents and Drs. should not be able to restrain babies, and take by force, what is not theirs.

Brothers and Sisters in Christ;

John Hagee
P.O. Box 1400
San Antonio, Tx. 78295-1400

Routine Infant Circumcision

This is my second letter to you regarding this subject.

I am an attentive listener, and own many of your tapes. I enjoy your dissertations concerning sex and marriage. My husband and I firmly believe in the perfection of God's plan for us. That his creation of the human body, both male and female, are perfectly matched to provide mutual pleasure, and fulfillment.

However this creation has been corrupted by man. That in the circumcising of the male prepuce, we have lost much of our natural, God-given right to sexual pleasure. Circumcision so interferes with the sexual responses of both men and women, that we have become enemies in our own bed. You profess that sex is the due benevolence of the marriage union, but fail to recognize the women's right to due benevolence. Pleasure for the women has been denied by the surgical alteration of our men, and we cannot experience the full measure of OUR rightful payment.

This IS the reason for the sexual discord in marriage. This IS the reason men and women are at odds when we argue and manipulate each other in the sexual theater of our relationships. Men continue to want sex on demand, and women use every reason under the sun to avoid it. The reason we try to avoid it is because sex is not satisfying, it is not the romantic closeness we expect. It has become a harsh act of penetration that involves pleasure for one partner only. Routine infant circumcision significantly interferes with the natural mechanics of sex. Women have been cheated from their rightful share of this due benevolence. We have been receiving a partial payment that is unacceptable, and unrewarding. The result is a withholding of sex, because of the discomfort and lack of fulfillment.

I strongly suggest that you consider the long term effects of genital mutilation, and the alteration of the natural act turned unnatural. Consider the sexual chaos we live in, and seek the answer to our problems in the routine perversion of our sex when are men are but babes in arms. Their pain and loss follows them far beyond the circumstraint board in the hospital, into our bedrooms, and then into the divorce courts of America.

Partial payment in any area of life is not acceptable, yet women have been, and are expected to respond naturally to an unnatural husband. This is unfair. We need men of your position to speak out for the protection of our future generations, and encourage people to respect the God-given bodies of their children, so that men and women of tomorrow will have all the necessary parts to make love as God intended. Man must stop mutilating the genitals of babies.

GERALD and LISA BISQUE

Surgeon General of the United States
HHH, 200 Independence Ave. SW
Washington, DC 20201

To: David Satcher M.D.,Ph.D.

Routine Infant Male Circumcision

I am concerned that the office of the Surgeon General
has not spoken out publicly against the practice of routine
infant male circumcision. I am not well informed of your
duties and responsibilities, and may be falsely accusatory.
The practice of infant circumcision is very widespread in
our country. It clearly is a violation of an individuals rights
and freedoms. To continue to allow parents and physicians
the power of genital mutilation over a completely helpless
individual, is at the very least barbaric. All babies cry out in
protest. Simply because they cannot form words that threat
retribution, and litigation, does not mean they are willing
participants. Since circumcision is a surgical procedure,
and you are the highest ranking surgeon in this country, it
makes perfect sense that you speak out for the protection of
the innocent.

It is the right thing to do. There are so many of us that resent having this thing forced on us, and the numbers are growing. We feel betrayed and violated. We feel, and rightly so, that something precious has been taken from us. This something, is not something that we would have given up freely. Sexual integrity is a birthright, and should be respected. Just as we expect our constitution to protect us from the bonds of slavery, we also expect protection from the unwanted mutilation of our sex organs.

A baby is a person. A baby boy will grow to be a man. A man that will be expected to perform at a certain level of proficiency when the time comes for him to be sexually active. Men in America have been denied even footing in this area because of infant circumcision. Baby girls grow into women. Women that will expect pleasure and satisfaction from making love with their men, and why shouldn't we? Yet we are lost in this life. Our men have been damaged, now we are both in pain.

We are holding up our end of the bargain. We work and pay taxes. We abide by the law of the land. We send our young into the military service. The very least we should expect in return is the right to grow up whole. It is too late for those that have already been subjected to this horror. I implore you to consider the future. You have the power, you can be the harbinger of a gentler, kinder, passage for the newborn American male.

You can be a hero. You can support the right of the newborn to be whole, to be free from the tether of ritualistic pain and terror. You are a powerful person, and I am certain that you will be remembered well for your benevolence. History will record your name as the one that brought enlightenment and true freedom to a people enslaved by darkness and pain.

Or, history can record your name as one who did nothing. Along with the rest of your contemporary predecessors, who also did nothing to stop the pain and permanent disfigurement of the American male genitalia. Rest assured that someone's name will be remembered kindly. Let it be yours.

Sincerely,

Gerald and Lisa Bisque

Dear Ms. Bisque:

Thank you for your June 28 letter regarding your concern about male circumcision. Medical practice in the United States is guided by professional medical organizations. The Nation has felt that the federal government should not direct how individual medical care decisions are made; rather, these choices should be determined by the individual patient and their health care provider.

The medical appropriateness of male infant circumcision has engendered ongoing discussions among health organizations over the last several decades. The American Acedemy of pedeatrics (AAP) and the American College of Obstetrics and Gynecologists both have policy statements on this subject. Beginning in 1975, AAP held that "There is no absolute medical indication for routine circumcision of the newborn." The Academy has modified its statement several times since then. The most recent conclusion reads:

"Existing scientific evidence demonstrates potential medical benefits of newborn male circumcision; however these data are not sufficient to recommend routine neonatal circumcision. In the case of circumcision, in which there are potential benefits and risks, yet the procedure is not essential to the child's current well-being, parents should determine what is in the best interest of the child…"

We anticipate that this revised policy statement will guide the pediatric health care community in the United States.

Sincerely Yours
David Satcher, M.D., Ph.D.
Assistant Secretary for Health and Surgeon General

Governor Jeb Bush
Tallahassee, Fl.

Dear Sir:

I am writing in protest of a common, and accepted medical practice that is descimating our culture. I am writing in protest of routine infant male circumcision. This procedure has robbed an entire generation and their children of the right to grow up whole. Our infant sons are subjected to a most painfull, disfiguring, surgical procedure performed on their genitals. This is done without their consent. The babies are completely vulnerable and susceptible to any attack that may advance.

The law is designed to protect its' citizens from harm. Yet in this most offensive of attacks, the law is completely impotent. There is no protection, and no sympathy. The ritualistic, medical mutilation of the infant male's genitals is a common, everyday occurrence. I can not understand why this is.

Our society decrys the unjust treatment of humans and animals, yet our own newborn sons are given into the hands of those that will hurt them. No law, and no protection.

People are beccoming more and more aware of this practice. They are beginning to understand what was done to them, and what the loss means to them. This new awareness will also awaken feelings of betrayal, violation, and assault. These feelings are going to be difficult to come to terms with. I see a society grieving, in pain and inconsolable. We have been taught to revere freedom and justice, and we were tied down and cut. Cut, sliced, lacerated, pinched, crushed, torn, and maimed. How do you tell someone this was for their own good?

We wouldn't stand for an animal to endure this. Yet nearly every American male is made to endure a painfull, permanently scarring, disfiguring, medical intervention.

The time to speak out for those that have no voice, is now. The babies are in danger of being hurt, and changed forever. Pain relief is not the answer. A total ban on the routine mutilation of a minors' genitals, is the only course.

Your position of power enables you to influence, and enforce the law of the land, which already protects it's citizens to life and liberty. Be the voice of reason and compassion. Let history record your name as the one that spoke out for the sexual integrity of Americans, and the protector of the innocent.

Sincerely,
        Gerald and Lisa Bisque

Letter to Cosmo

I am a 41 y/o w/f. I have had the most unfortunate opportunity to grow and live in a society that has routinely circumcised its male citizens in their infancy. The price we pay for this anti-sexual activity, is the permanent loss of our natural sexuality, the breaking of the natural love bond between men and women. This re-constructing of the male penis has brought us to war with each other, and the battle rages in our bedrooms. Sexual intercourse is not the intimate, loving, satisfying closeness we all expected, but rather a coarse, quick ramming, caused by the lack of foreskin, which nature intended, to facilitate a smooth gliding action that would result in a more comfortable, enjoyable experience. Your recent article describing the so-called C-spot as an erogenous zone that should make one grateful for being circumcised is insulting. The very act of forced removal of erogenous tissue is a criminal act of assault, and the foreskin is highly erogenous, and necessary for the mutual enjoyment of sexual intercourse. The C-spot is nothing more than evidence of sexual assault, the scar tissue that remains as a constant reminder of a person's helplessness and vulnerability at a tender age. I think that your magazine has an obligation to be truthfull regarding sexual function and specifically informative about the loss incurred by both partners when it comes to the surgical alteration of the male penis.

Sincerely Disssatisfied With Circumcision In America: Lisa Bisque

www.ingramcontent.com/pod-product-compliance
Lightning Source LLC
Chambersburg PA
CBHW020250290526
45784CB00003B/1181